Looking at the Sky

To my big sister, Erika—J.F.

Library of Congress Cataloging-in-Publication Data is available.

ISBN 0-448-42488-6   A B C D E F G H I J

MY FIRST FIELD GUIDE

Looking at the Sky

By Jennifer Frantz

Illustrated by Pedro Julio Gonzalez
and Tim Haggerty

Grosset & Dunlap • New York

Scientists study the sky all the time.
But did you know that you
can study the sky, too?

When can you
sky watch?
You can look
at the sky anytime—
day or night!
There are cool things
in the sky all
of the time.

This book shows you what to look for. It also has stickers! They will help you keep track of what you see. When you identify something from the book, just put its sticker on that page and write down the date you saw it. You can also use the blank pages in the back of the book to write down what you see.

Here's what you may need

Day watching

Sunglasses

Sunscreen

Notebook and pencil

Compass

Binoculars

A blanket or folding chair

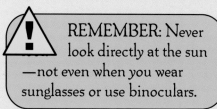

REMEMBER: Never look directly at the sun —not even when you wear sunglasses or use binoculars.

Night watching

A flashlight covered with red plastic wrap or acetate (By making your flashlight less bright, you will see more in the sky!)

Notebook and pencil

Compass

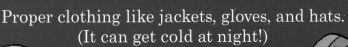

Binoculars and/or telescope

Proper clothing like jackets, gloves, and hats. (It can get cold at night!)

A blanket or folding chair

Sky watching with somebody else along is twice the fun!

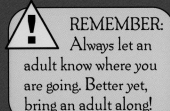

! REMEMBER: Always let an adult know where you are going. Better yet, bring an adult along!

The Sun

The sun is a star.
But you see it in the day.
You can't see other stars
in the day. Why?
Because the sun is
the star closest to us.
Its light looks the brightest.

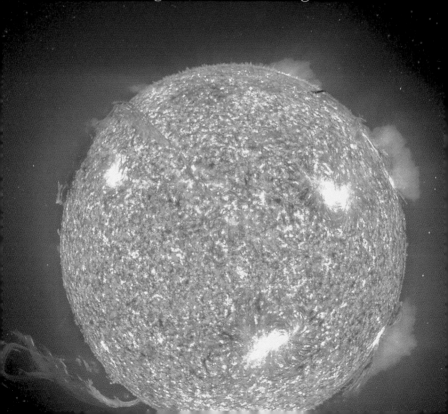

The light from the sun
keeps our planet alive.
It keeps the earth warm.
Without the sun,
there would be no plants,
animals, or people on Earth.

Long ago, people thought the sun orbited the Earth. Now we know that the Earth circles around the sun.

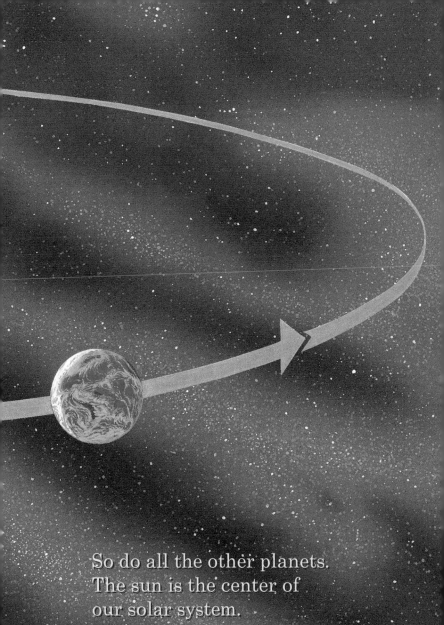

So do all the other planets.
The sun is the center of
our solar system.

Sunrise and Sunset

Every day the sun rises in the east. And every day the sun sets in the west.

So when you look for a sunrise, find east on your compass. When you look for a sunset, find west on your compass.

Going, going, gone . . . You've got to be quick to catch a sunset. Once the sun touches the horizon, it takes less than 2 minutes to disappear!

But the time of the sunrise and the sunset changes every day. In the winter, there is less daylight.
The sun rises later and sets earlier.
In the summer, daylight lasts longer.
The sun rises earlier
and sets later.

5 pm in winter

5 pm in summer

Sunrise and sunset times also depend on where you live. Check a newspaper, or the Internet, for daily sunrise and sunset times.

I saw the
sunset

place your
sticker here

During the day,
the sun moves across the sky.
It moves from east to west in an arc.
In ancient times, people used the sun
to tell time. You can try to tell time
using the sun, too. At noon,
the sun is at its highest point in the
sky. In the morning, the sun is closer
to the east. In the afternoon,
it has moved to the west.

What Time Is It?

Use the diagram on the facing page
to help you guess the time.

1. Find the position of the sun in the sky.

2. Make your guess.

3. Then, check your watch.

The more you
try, the better
you'll get!

REMEMBER:
Wear sunglasses and never
look directly at the sun!

Clouds

Everyone has seen a cloud.
But did you ever wonder
what a cloud is made of?
Or why clouds are different shapes?

I see a bone.

Clouds are made
of very tiny water drops
in the air. Hot air acts like a sponge.
It pulls water from rivers, lakes, ponds,
and oceans. Once the water is in the
air, it cools. This makes a cloud.

There are three main types of clouds.
They are different shapes.

Cumulus Clouds
Cumulus (you say it: cume YOU luss)
are big and puffy.

You see them on nice, warm days.
Why do they look so white?
Because sunlight bounces off
all the teeny water drops.
Look for them in the summer.

I saw a
**cumulus
cloud**

place your
sticker here

Look for cirrus clouds on windy days.

Cirrus Clouds
Cirrus (you say it: sear US)
are wispy and thin.
They are very high
up in the sky.
It is very cold there.
The water drops freeze
into tiny ice crystals.
Wind blows the tiny ice pieces
into odd shapes.

I saw a
**cirrus
cloud**

place your
sticker here

Look for
stratus clouds
on gloomy days.

Stratus Clouds

Stratus (you say it: strat US)
are flat gray clouds.
They cover the sky like a blanket.
They block the sun from view.
Stratus clouds often mean
snow or rain is coming!

I saw a
**stratus
cloud**

place your
sticker here

Rainbows

You can only see rainbows after it rains. Why? Because rainbows are made of water drops and light.

How does rain make rainbows? Sunlight shines through water drops in the air. The water breaks up the different colors in the light, like a prism.

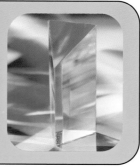

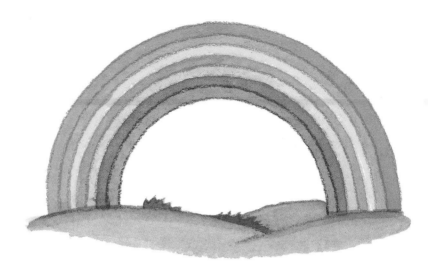

Here are some rainbow hunting tips:

1. The sun should be at your back.

2. Look when the sun is low in the sky.

3. Check near other "rain" sources— like sprinklers and waterfalls.

I saw a
rainbow

place your
sticker here

Make a Rainbow

If you can't find a rainbow—make one!

1. Fill a shallow
pan with water.

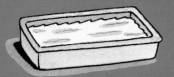

2. Set the pan near
a window with lots
of sunlight.

3. Now hold a small
mirror inside the pan.

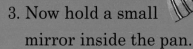

4. Look for your
rainbow on the wall!

The Moon

The moon circles around Earth. The moon is much smaller than earth. If the moon were a golf ball, the earth would be a tennis ball. The moon does not make its own light. It shines because sunlight hits it. It acts like a mirror. But the moon is not really shiny—it is made of rock.

surface of the moon

Moon Myths

○ The moon is made of cheese.
○ There's a man in the moon.

Both of these moon myths are totally false!
How did these myths start?
The moon's surface is covered with craters.
From far away, it can look like holes—like
Swiss cheese. Or, even faces—like the man
in the moon!

It takes the moon one month
to orbit once around the Earth.
During this time, the moon looks
like it changes shape. The different
shapes are called phases.

At the beginning
of the month,
it looks like
a skinny banana.
This is a new moon.

Then it gets
bigger…and bigger!
This is called waxing.

By the middle of the month, it looks like a big ball. That is a full moon. The moon goes from new to full in two weeks.

Then it gets smaller...and smaller! This is called waning.

It goes from full back down to new. This takes another two weeks.

My Moon Calendar

Now you can keep track
of the moon's phases—
using the moon stickers
in the front of the book.

1. Go outside and
   look at the moon.

2. Find the sticker
   that looks like
   what you see.

4. Write the date
   below the sticker.

5. Do this every four
   days for a month.

3. Put the sticker on your calendar.

When your chart is done, you should see the pattern of the moon's "waxing" and "waning". This way, you can see for yourself how the moon's phases work!

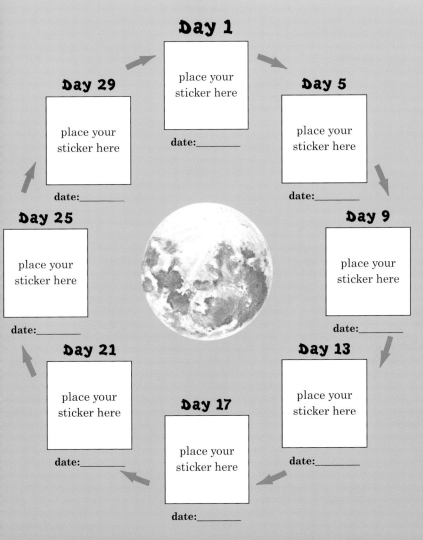

Stars

People love looking at stars.
But what is a star?
A star is a big,
bright ball of gas.

There are billions
and billions of stars in space.
They are millions of miles
away from Earth.
Many are bigger than our sun.

Seeing Stars

Some nights, you can see
thousands of stars.
Some nights, only a few.
Why is that?

One reason is light pollution.
This means that other lights in cities
make it harder to see stars.

Star Light, Star Bright

Here's an experiment to try:

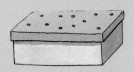

1. Poke some holes in the top of a shoebox. (These holes will be your stars!)

2. Turn on your flashlight and put it in the shoebox.

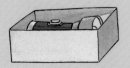

3. Go into a closet.

4. Shut the door and see how bright your stars look.

5. Now open the closet door a crack to let outside light in.

Your stars look less bright don't they? This is light pollution!

One of the easiest stars to find
is the North Star. It is also called
Polaris (you say it: po lair ess).
Polaris never moves. It is always right
above the North Pole.

It is also very bright. Sailors used to use it to navigate their ships. You can use Polaris to help you find north in the night sky.

If you find
Polaris, you
can find the
"Dippers."
The Big Dipper
and the
Little Dipper
are constellations
(You say it:
con sta lay shun).
Since ancient
times, people
have seen
these dot-to-dot
pictures in
the stars.

The Big Dipper is
right next to the
Little Dipper.

I saw the
**Big
Dipper**

place your
sticker here

The North Star (Polaris)
is at the very end of
the Little Dipper's
handle.

They both look like soup ladles.
The only difference is their size.
Both Dippers can be seen
all year round. But they are
in different parts of the sky
at different times of the year.
They revolve around Polaris.

I saw the
Little
Dipper

place your
sticker here

Orion

Another good constellation
to find is Orion (you say it: or eye on).

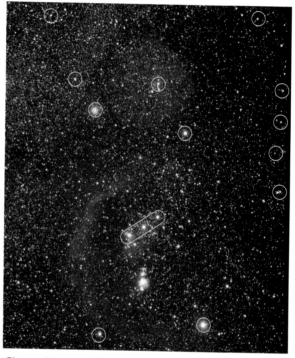

In Greek myths, Orion was a mighty
hunter. He bragged that he could kill
any animal. This made the gods
angry. Orion was cast into the sky
with his shield and club.

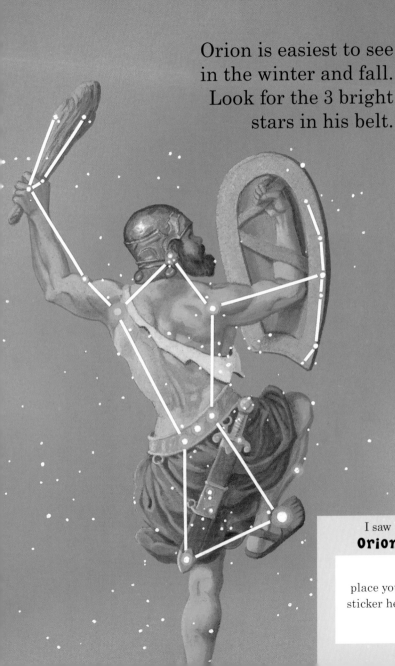

Orion is easiest to see in the winter and fall. Look for the 3 bright stars in his belt.

I saw
Orion

place your
sticker here

Some stars you see may really
be planets! You can't see all
9 planets. But if you're lucky,
you can see 4 of them—
Venus, Jupiter, Mars,
and Saturn.

How do you know it's a
planet, not a star? Planets
don't twinkle like stars.
They also look a bit bigger
and brighter. But you
will have to look <u>very</u> closely
to find them. (A telescope
or binoculars can help!)

Jupiter

Saturn

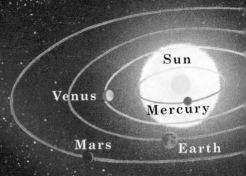

Venus is sometimes called the evening star. Aside from the moon, it is the brightest body in the night sky.

Jupiter and Saturn also look brighter than stars. But they are not as bright as Venus. Mars has a reddish color— even from far away.

I saw a
planet

place your
sticker here

Even if you can't see them all—
all 9 planets are special. Like Earth,
they all orbit around the sun.
They make up our solar system.

 Mercury is the planet closest
to the sun. It is very hot!

Venus is called Earth's twin.
They are almost the same size.
Venus is <u>very</u> hot and dry and
has volcanoes.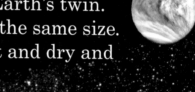

 **Earth** is known as the blue
planet. Water covers about
$\frac{2}{3}$ of its surface!

Mars is the red planet.
Its surface is covered
with dust—not aliens!

Jupiter is the biggest planet
in our solar system. Its giant
red spot is a huge storm two
times as big as Earth!

Saturn is famous for its rings. They are made of tiny pieces of ice and dust.

Uranus is the third largest planet. It is made mostly of gas. It is blue-green in color.

Neptune is almost the same size as Uranus. It also shares its blue-green color.

Pluto is the smallest planet. It is also the farthest from the sun.

"My Very Energetic Mother Just Served Us Nine Pickles"
This silly sentence can help you remember the planets: Mercury, Venus, Earth, Mars, Jupiter, Saturn, Uranus, Neptune, Pluto

Meteors

You have probably heard of a shooting star. Maybe you've even seen one. But did you know that shooting stars are <u>not</u> stars? They are meteors (you say it: meaty orz). Meteors are space rocks. When they fall toward Earth, they burn up. This burning streak is what we see. When a lot of meteors fall toward Earth, it is called a meteor shower.

Some meteor showers happen around the same time every year. Look for meteors on these nights:

January 2–4	August 10–13
April 20–22	October 8–10
May 4–6	October 18–23
July 26–28	November 8–10
December 10–13	

You will have to look very carefully to see one. Meteors are very fast!

I saw a
meteor

place your
sticker here

Comets

If you are very lucky, you might see a comet. Comets are known as dirty snowballs. They are made of dirt, ice, and gas.

A comet looks like a fuzzy ball with a tail.

The tail is made when the comet flies around the sun. The hot sun melts the ice which makes the tail. Some comets visit regularly. Halley's Comet, for example, comes every 76 years. To find out when you can see a comet, look on the Internet, or contact a science or space museum.

I saw a
comet

place your
sticker here

People are always learning more
and more about the sky and space.

There are always new things to see.
Visit a museum or a planetarium to find
out even more about the sky and space.
You never know what you'll see
when you look up!

Looking at the Sky

My Field Notes

*Use these pages to write down or draw what you see when you are looking at the sky.

Today's date:

Time of day (circle one):

morning   afternoon   evening   night

My notes:

You can draw here!

Today's date: _____

Time of day (circle one):

    morning   afternoon   evening   night

My notes:

You can draw here!

Today's date:

Time of day (circle one):

morning afternoon evening night

My notes:

You can draw here!

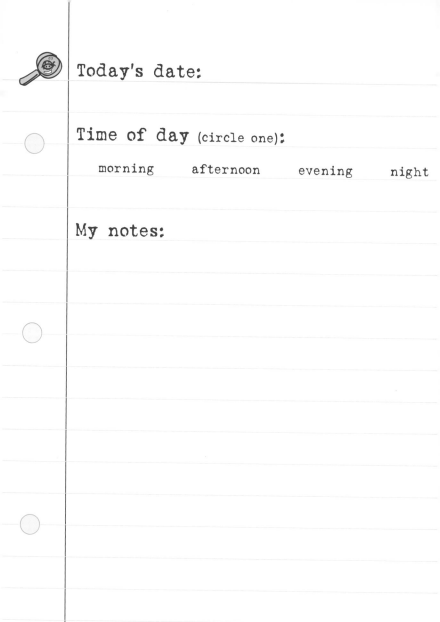

Today's date: _____

Time of day (circle one):

morning   afternoon   evening   night

My notes:

You can draw here!

Today's date: _____

Time of day (circle one):

    morning   afternoon   evening   night

My notes:

You can draw here!

Today's date: _____

Time of day (circle one):

    morning   afternoon   evening   night

My notes:

You can draw here!

Today's date: _____

Time of day (circle one):

    morning   afternoon   evening   night

My notes:

You can draw here!

More Notes: